Dry As a Desert

by Libby Romero

Table of Contents

Introduction

Look at all the **deserts**. How are they alike? How are they different?

1. Mojave Desert, North America

2. Atacama Desert, South America

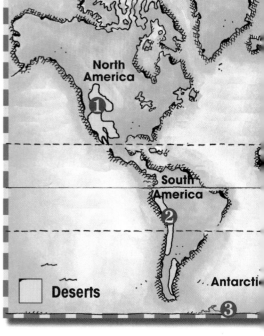

North America

1

South America

2

☐ **Deserts**

Antarcti

3

3. Antarctica

4. Sahara Desert, Africa

2

6. Gobi Desert, Asia

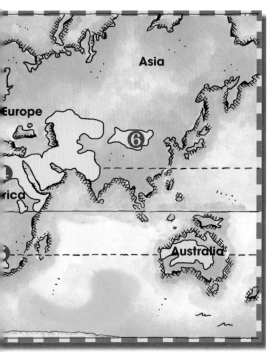

Europe

Asia

⑥

rica

Australia

5. Namib Desert, Africa

adapt

coast

deserts

dunes

shade

See the Glossary
on page 22.

What Are Deserts?

Deserts are very dry places.

Some deserts are hot.

S O lve This!

There are two ways to measure temperature, Fahrenheit and Celsius.

To change a temperature from Fahrenheit to Celsius, subtract 32 and then divide by 1.8.

Use this formula to change the hottest temperature in the Sahara to Celsius.

Answer: 57.8°

▲ The hottest temperature in the Sahara Desert was 136°F.

Some deserts are cold.

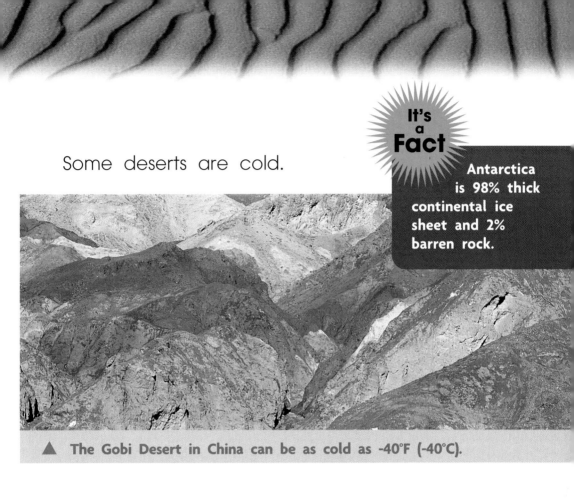

▲ The Gobi Desert in China can be as cold as -40°F (-40°C).

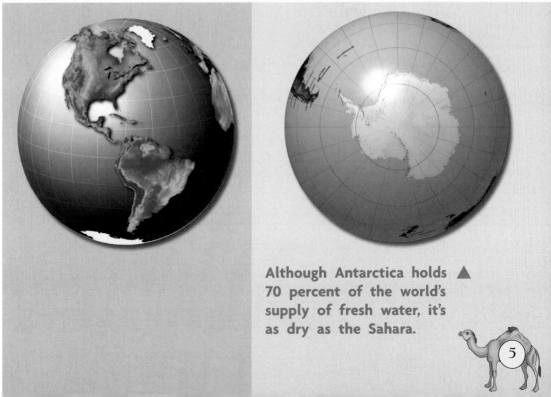

Although Antarctica holds ▲ 70 percent of the world's supply of fresh water, it's as dry as the Sahara.

Some deserts have sand. Wind blows the sand into big piles. The piles are called **dunes**.

▲ Some dunes in the Sahara Desert are more than 600 feet (180 meters) high.

▲ Some deserts have rocks.

▲ Some deserts have gravel.

▲ Some deserts have salt.

▲ Some deserts have beautiful shapes.

Where Are Deserts?

Deserts are all over the world.

▲ The Gobi Desert covers 500,000 square miles (1.3 million square kilometers).

Some deserts are far from oceans.
Those deserts stay dry all the time.

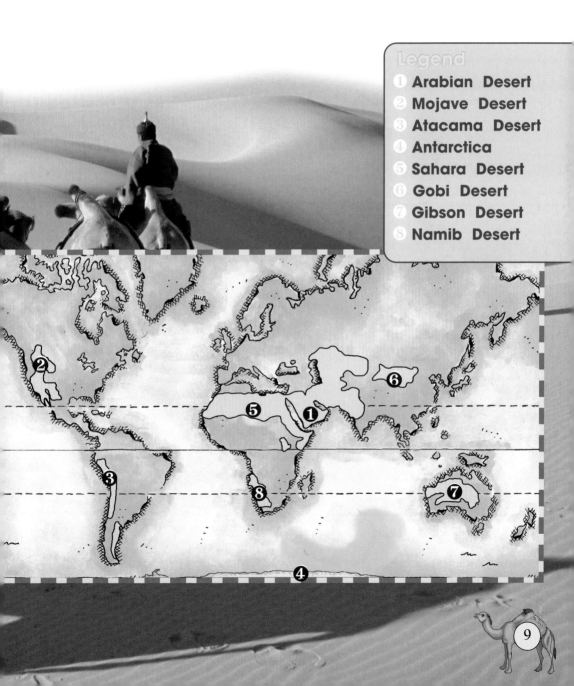

Legend
① Arabian Desert
② Mojave Desert
③ Atacama Desert
④ Antarctica
⑤ Sahara Desert
⑥ Gobi Desert
⑦ Gibson Desert
⑧ Namib Desert

Some deserts are next to mountains. Rain falls on one side of the mountains. The rain cannot get over the mountains. The other side stays dry.

▲ The Sangre de Cristo Mountains are behind these dunes.

Some deserts are on the **coast**. Sometimes there is fog. There is not much rain.

TryThis

The temperature in the Sahara Desert can be 50 degrees cooler at night than it is during the day.

Every day for a week,

- Write the highest temperature during the day where you live;

- Write the lowest temperature at night where you live;

- Write the difference between the two temperatures for each day.

Is the difference in the temperatures you wrote down greater than the difference in the Sahara temperatures? By how much?

Is the difference in your temperatures less than the difference in the Sahara temperatures? By how much?

▲ It is a foggy morning in the Namib Desert.

Some deserts are in hot places. Winds blow very hot, dry air there.

North America

Asia

Europe

Africa

South America

Australia

Antarctica

It's a Fact

The Sahara was not always a desert. It was covered with grasses and bushes 5,000 years ago.

▲ The Sahara Desert has hot, dry air.

13

What Lives in Deserts?
Who Lives in Deserts?

▲ Desert plants start to grow after it rains.

Many plants live in deserts. They **adapt**, or change. They can live without much water.

▲ This tree keeps water in its trunk.

▲ This cactus grows when it rains.

15

Many animals live in deserts. Most desert animals are small. They find **shade** under rocks and plants. Bigger animals find other ways to stay cool.

▲ Desert elephants cool themselves with dust.

▲ Snakes hide in the shade to survive the heat.

16

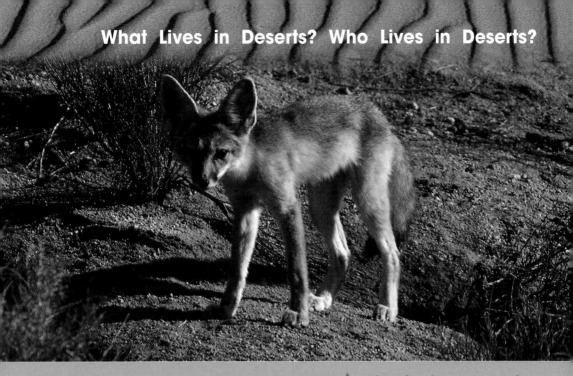

▲ This fox hunts at night.

Many desert animals come out at night. It is not hot. They can find food then.

It's a Fact!

Camels have nostrils that open and close. They have bushy eyebrows and long eyelashes. These protect camels from the sand.

17

People live in deserts, too. There are big cities in some deserts.

Many large desert buildings are made of mud bricks.

People learn to use desert plants.

Learn More

To learn more about plants and animals that live in the desert, visit this Web site: www.enchantedlearning.com/ biomes/desert/desert.shtml.

People often live in small groups in the desert. People learn to live in the desert.

19

All deserts are dry. Deserts look different. Deserts are in different places.

Deserts

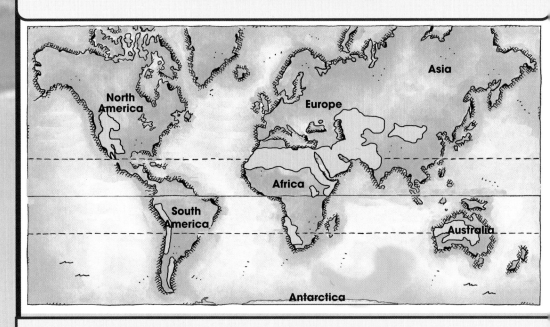

Asia

North America

Europe

Africa

South America

Australia

Antarctica

all over the world

Think About It

1. What is a desert?
2. Where are deserts?
3. What lives in deserts?

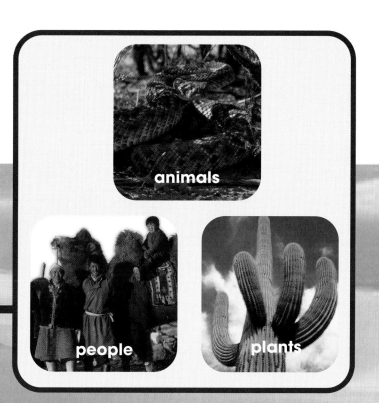

animals

people

plants

gravel

salt

sand

rocks

21

Glossary

adapt to change

*Camels **adapt** to blowing sand and hot weather.*

coast the land beside an ocean

*Some deserts are on the **coast.***

deserts very dry places

*It never rains in parts of some **deserts.***

dunes piles of sand made by the wind

*The Sahara desert has many large **dunes.***

shade out of the sunshine

It is cool in the shade.

Index